I0017720

Artificial Intelligence and Machine Learning

Franklin Fisher

 Published by Amazon KDP

Amazon.com, Inc.

P.O. Box 81226

Seattle, WA 98108-1226

United States.

Printed by Amazon KDP in the USA

Table of Contents

FRANKLIN FISHER.. I

TABLE OF CONTENTS.. III

CHAPTER 1 1

INTRODUCTION TO THE AI REVOLUTION 1

DEFINING AI AND MACHINE LEARNING..............1
HISTORICAL OVERVIEW: FROM EARLY
CONCEPTS TO MODERN ADVANCEMENTS...........2
THE IMPACT OF AI ON SOCIETY AND INDUSTRY.3

CHAPTER 2 5

FOUNDATIONS OF MACHINE LEARNING 5

UNDERSTANDING DATA: THE LIFEBLOOD OF
MACHINE LEARNING..5
SUPERVISED, UNSUPERVISED, AND
REINFORCEMENT LEARNING 6
FEATURE ENGINEERING AND DIMENSIONALITY
REDUCTION..7
MODEL EVALUATION AND VALIDATION
TECHNIQUES...9

CHAPTER 3 11

DEEP DIVE INTO NEURAL NETWORKS 11

NEURONS AND ACTIVATION FUNCTIONS...........11
ARCHITECTURES: FROM PERCEPTRONS TO
CONVOLUTIONAL AND RECURRENT NEURAL
NETWORKS 12

TRAINING NEURAL NETWORKS:
BACKPROPAGATION AND OPTIMIZATION
ALGORITHMS 13
OVERFITTING, REGULARIZATION, AND DROPOUT
.... 14

CHAPTER 4 .... **16**

THE POWER OF DEEP LEARNING **16**

IMAGE RECOGNITION AND COMPUTER VISION 16
NATURAL LANGUAGE PROCESSING AND TEXT
ANALYSIS 17

CHAPTER 5 .... **19**

ETHICS AND BIAS IN AI 19
UNDERSTANDING BIAS AND FAIRNESS IN
MACHINE LEARNING 19
AI AND PRIVACY: BALANCING INNOVATION
WITH PERSONAL DATA PROTECTION 20
THE ROLE OF REGULATION AND GOVERNANCE
IN AI DEVELOPMENT 21

CHAPTER 6 .... **23**

REINFORCEMENT LEARNING AND AUTONOMOUS
SYSTEMS 23
MARKOV DECISION PROCESSES AND Q-
LEARNING 23
APPLICATIONS IN ROBOTICS, GAMING, AND
SELF-DRIVING CARS 24
CHALLENGES AND FUTURE DIRECTIONS IN
REINFORCEMENT LEARNING 25

CHAPTER 7 .... **27**

AI FOR GOOD: SOLVING GLOBAL CHALLENGES
....27
AI IN HUMANITARIAN AID AND DISASTER
RESPONSE 27
ENVIRONMENTAL SUSTAINABILITY AND
CLIMATE CHANGE MITIGATION........................28
HEALTHCARE AND DISEASE DIAGNOSIS............30

CHAPTER 8 ....**32**

THE FUTURE OF AI: TRENDS AND SPECULATIONS
....32
QUANTUM COMPUTING AND AI..........................32
EXPLAINABLE AI: MAKING ALGORITHMS
UNDERSTANDABLE 33
THE EMERGENCE OF ARTIFICIAL GENERAL
INTELLIGENCE (AGI)...34
ETHICAL CONSIDERATIONS IN FUTURE AI
DEVELOPMENT 35

CHAPTER 9 ....**38**

BUILDING YOUR AI JOURNEY............................38
EDUCATION AND SKILL DEVELOPMENT IN AI
AND MACHINE LEARNING 38
TOOLS AND FRAMEWORKS FOR AI
DEVELOPMENT 39
COLLABORATIVE PROJECTS AND OPEN SOURCE
COMMUNITIES 41

CHAPTER 10 ....**43**

CONCLUSION: EMBRACING THE AI ODYSSEY...43
REFLECTIONS ON THE EVOLUTION OF AI AND
ITS IMPACTS 43

CALL TO ACTION: SHAPING A RESPONSIBLE AND
INCLUSIVE AI FUTURE 44
THE ENDLESS POSSIBILITIES AND LIMITLESS
POTENTIAL OF ARTIFICIAL INTELLIGENCE 45

Chapter 1

Introduction to the AI Revolution

Artificial Intelligence (AI) is the culmination of humanity's age-old quest to create machines that can think, learn, and act autonomously. It represents a technological revolution that is reshaping industries, societies, and the very fabric of human existence. At the heart of this revolution lies Machine Learning, a subset of AI that empowers computers to learn from data and improve over time without explicit programming.

Defining AI and Machine Learning

AI encompasses a broad range of techniques and approaches aimed at creating intelligent systems capable of performing tasks that typically require human intelligence. These tasks include reasoning, problem-solving, perception, understanding natural language, and learning from experience. Machine Learning, a core component of AI, focuses on developing algorithms and models that allow computers to learn patterns and make predictions from data.

Historical Overview: From Early Concepts to Modern Advancements

The roots of AI can be traced back to ancient times, with myths and legends featuring artificial beings imbued with human-like intelligence. However, the modern concept of AI emerged in the mid-20th century, with seminal works such as Alan Turing's Turing Test and the Dartmouth Conference in 1956, where the term "artificial intelligence" was coined.

Early AI research focused on symbolic approaches, where explicit rules and logic were used to simulate human reasoning. However, progress was slow, and AI faced significant challenges due to limitations in computing power and data availability.

The advent of Machine Learning in the late 20th century revolutionized the field of AI. Instead of relying on handcrafted rules,

Machine Learning algorithms could learn patterns and relationships directly from data. Breakthroughs in neural networks, such as the perceptron and backpropagation algorithm, paved the way for the rise of Deep Learning—a subfield of Machine Learning that utilizes large neural networks with many layers to achieve remarkable results in tasks such as image recognition, natural language processing, and game playing.

The Impact of AI on Society and Industry

The proliferation of AI technologies is reshaping society and transforming industries across the globe. From virtual assistants and recommendation systems to autonomous vehicles and medical diagnosis, AI is becoming increasingly ubiquitous in our daily lives.

In healthcare, AI-powered diagnostic tools are revolutionizing disease detection and treatment planning, leading to improved patient outcomes and more personalized care. In finance, AI algorithms are used for fraud detection, risk assessment, and algorithmic trading, enhancing efficiency and reducing human error.

However, the widespread adoption of AI also raises concerns about job displacement, privacy violations, and ethical implications. As AI systems become more autonomous and pervasive, it is crucial to address these challenges and ensure that AI technologies are developed and deployed responsibly, ethically, and inclusively.

As we embark on this AI revolution, it is essential to understand the fundamentals of AI and Machine Learning, appreciate their historical context, and critically examine their impact on society and industry. Only by doing so can we navigate the opportunities and challenges that lie ahead and harness the transformative power of AI for the betterment of humanity.

Chapter 2

Foundations of Machine Learning

Machine Learning (ML) is the driving force behind many of the remarkable achievements in Artificial Intelligence (AI). In this chapter, we will delve into the fundamental concepts that underpin Machine Learning, from understanding data to evaluating and validating models.

Understanding Data: The Lifeblood of Machine Learning

Data is the cornerstone of Machine Learning. It fuels the training process, allowing algorithms to learn patterns and make predictions. Understanding the characteristics of data is crucial for building effective ML models.

- **Types of Data**: Data can be categorized into various types, including numerical, categorical, ordinal, and text data. Each type requires different preprocessing techniques and model architectures.

- **Data Preprocessing**: Before feeding data into ML models, it often requires preprocessing steps such as cleaning, normalization, and encoding categorical variables. These steps ensure that the data is in a suitable format for training.
- **Exploratory Data Analysis (EDA)**: EDA involves analyzing and visualizing the data to gain insights into its distribution, relationships, and potential patterns. This step helps in feature selection and understanding the underlying structure of the data.

Supervised, Unsupervised, and Reinforcement Learning

Machine Learning tasks can be broadly categorized into three types: supervised, unsupervised, and reinforcement learning.

- **Supervised Learning**: In supervised learning, the algorithm learns from labeled data, where each example is associated with a corresponding target or output. The goal is to learn a mapping from input to output, enabling the model to make predictions on unseen data.

- **Unsupervised Learning**: Unsupervised learning deals with unlabeled data, where the algorithm aims to find hidden patterns or structures in the data. Clustering, dimensionality reduction, and anomaly detection are common tasks in unsupervised learning.

- **Reinforcement Learning**: Reinforcement learning involves training an agent to interact with an environment and learn optimal actions through trial and error. The agent receives feedback in the form of rewards or penalties based on its actions, guiding its learning process.

Feature Engineering and Dimensionality Reduction

Feature engineering is the process of selecting, transforming, and creating features from raw data to improve the performance of ML models.

- **Feature Selection**: Identifying the most relevant features that contribute to the predictive power of the model while reducing noise and overfitting.
- **Feature Transformation**: Transforming features to make them more suitable for the model, such as scaling numerical features or encoding categorical variables.
- **Feature Creation**: Generating new features by combining or transforming existing ones to capture additional information from the data.

Dimensionality reduction techniques aim to reduce the number of features in the dataset while preserving as much relevant information as possible.

- **Principal Component Analysis (PCA)**: PCA is a popular technique for reducing the dimensionality of data by finding orthogonal axes (principal components) that capture the maximum variance in the data.
- **t-Distributed Stochastic Neighbor Embedding (t-SNE)**: t-SNE is a nonlinear dimensionality reduction technique commonly used for visualizing high-dimensional data in

lower-dimensional space while preserving local structure.

Model Evaluation and Validation Techniques

Evaluating and validating ML models is essential to ensure their effectiveness and generalization to unseen data.

- **Train-Test Split**: Splitting the dataset into training and testing sets to evaluate the model's performance on unseen data.
- **Cross-Validation**: Dividing the data into multiple subsets (folds) and training the model on different combinations of folds to obtain robust performance estimates.
- **Metrics for Evaluation**: Metrics such as accuracy, precision, recall, F1-score, and area under the receiver operating characteristic curve (ROC AUC) are commonly used to evaluate classification models. For regression models, metrics such as mean squared error (MSE) and R-squared are used.

By mastering the foundations of Machine Learning, including understanding data, learning algorithms, feature engineering, and model evaluation, practitioners can build robust and effective ML models for a wide range of applications.

Chapter 3

Deep Dive into Neural Networks

Neural networks are the cornerstone of modern machine learning, enabling computers to learn complex patterns from data. In this chapter, we will explore the inner workings of neural networks, from their basic building blocks to advanced architectures and training techniques.

Neurons and Activation Functions

At the core of neural networks are artificial neurons, which mimic the functionality of biological neurons in the human brain. Each neuron receives input signals, processes them, and produces an output signal.

- **Neural Network Layers**: Neurons are organized into layers within a neural network. The input layer receives input data, the output layer produces the final output, and one or more hidden layers perform intermediate computations.

- **Activation Functions**: Activation functions introduce nonlinearity into the neural network, enabling it to learn complex mappings between inputs and outputs. Common activation functions include sigmoid, tanh, ReLU (Rectified Linear Unit), and softmax.

Architectures: From Perceptrons to Convolutional and Recurrent Neural Networks

Neural network architectures vary in complexity and are tailored to specific tasks and data types.

- **Perceptrons**: Perceptrons are the simplest form of neural networks, consisting of a single layer of neurons with binary outputs. They are the building blocks of more complex networks.
- **Convolutional Neural Networks (CNNs)**: CNNs are specialized neural networks designed for processing grid-like data, such as images. They

use convolutional layers to automatically learn spatial hierarchies of features.

- **Recurrent Neural Networks (RNNs)**: RNNs are designed to process sequences of data, such as time series or natural language. They have connections between neurons that form directed cycles, allowing them to retain information over time.

Training Neural Networks: Backpropagation and Optimization Algorithms

Training a neural network involves adjusting its parameters (weights and biases) to minimize a loss function, which measures the difference between predicted and actual outputs.

- **Backpropagation**: Backpropagation is a key algorithm for training neural networks. It works by iteratively adjusting the network's parameters in the opposite direction of the gradient of the loss function with respect to those parameters.
- **Optimization Algorithms**: Various optimization algorithms are used to

update the parameters during training, such as stochastic gradient descent (SGD), Adam, and RMSprop. These algorithms aim to find the optimal set of parameters that minimize the loss function efficiently.

Overfitting, Regularization, and Dropout

- **Overfitting** occurs when a neural network learns to memorize the training data instead of generalizing from it, leading to poor performance on unseen data.

- **Regularization**: Regularization techniques such as L1 and L2 regularization penalize large weights in the network, preventing overfitting and promoting simpler models.

- **Dropout**: Dropout is a technique where random neurons are temporarily dropped out (ignored) during training. This helps prevent overfitting by introducing redundancy and forcing the network to learn more robust features.

By understanding the principles of neural networks, including neurons and activation functions, different architectures, training algorithms, and techniques to prevent overfitting, practitioners can effectively design and train neural networks for a wide range of tasks and domains.

Chapter 4

The Power of Deep Learning

Deep Learning, a subset of Machine Learning, has revolutionized various fields by enabling computers to learn from large amounts of data with unprecedented accuracy and efficiency. In this chapter, we explore some of the most impactful applications of Deep Learning across different domains.

Image Recognition and Computer Vision

Deep Learning has significantly advanced the field of computer vision, enabling machines to understand and interpret visual information with human-like accuracy.

- **Image Classification**: Deep neural networks, particularly Convolutional Neural Networks (CNNs), have achieved remarkable success in classifying objects within images.

Applications range from identifying everyday objects to detecting abnormalities in medical images.

- **Object Detection and Localization**: Deep Learning models can localize and identify multiple objects within images, providing valuable information for tasks such as autonomous driving, surveillance, and augmented reality.

- **Semantic Segmentation**: Deep Learning techniques such as Fully Convolutional Networks (FCNs) can segment images into semantically meaningful regions, allowing for fine-grained understanding of visual scenes.

Natural Language Processing and Text Analysis

Deep Learning has transformed Natural Language Processing (NLP), enabling machines to understand, generate, and interact with human language.

- **Text Classification and Sentiment Analysis**: Deep Learning models, including Recurrent Neural Networks (RNNs) and Transformer architectures like BERT, are used for tasks such as sentiment analysis, document classification, and spam detection.

- **Machine Translation**: Deep Learning has revolutionized machine translation with models like Google's Neural Machine Translation (GNMT) and the Transformer architecture, achieving near-human levels of translation quality across multiple languages.
- **Named Entity Recognition and Text Generation**: Deep Learning models can extract named entities from text and generate

Chapter 5

Ethics and Bias in AI

As Artificial Intelligence (AI) becomes increasingly integrated into various aspects of society, it brings with it a myriad of ethical considerations and challenges. In this chapter, we delve into the critical issues of bias, fairness, privacy, and the role of regulation and governance in AI development.

Understanding Bias and Fairness in Machine Learning

Bias in AI refers to systematic errors or unfairness in the decision-making processes of AI systems, often stemming from biased training data or algorithmic design choices.

- **Types of Bias**: Bias can manifest in various forms, including demographic bias, where certain groups are disproportionately affected by AI decisions, and algorithmic bias, where the model's predictions are skewed towards specific outcomes.

- **Fairness Measures**: Researchers and practitioners are developing methods to quantify and mitigate bias in AI systems, such as fairness-aware machine learning algorithms and fairness metrics that assess the distribution of outcomes across different demographic groups.

AI and Privacy: Balancing Innovation with Personal Data Protection

AI systems often rely on vast amounts of personal data to train and operate effectively, raising concerns about privacy infringement and data misuse.

- **Data Privacy**: Data privacy regulations, such as the European Union's General Data Protection Regulation (GDPR) and the California Consumer Privacy Act (CCPA), aim to protect individuals' rights to privacy and control over their personal data.
- **Privacy-Preserving Techniques**: Privacy-preserving techniques, including federated learning,

differential privacy, and homomorphic encryption, enable AI models to be trained and deployed without directly accessing sensitive user data.

The Role of Regulation and Governance in AI Development

Effective regulation and governance are essential to ensure that AI technologies are developed and deployed responsibly, ethically, and inclusively.

- **Ethical Guidelines**: Organizations such as the IEEE, ACM, and Partnership on AI have developed ethical guidelines and principles to guide the responsible development and use of AI technologies.
- **Government Regulation**: Governments around the world are beginning to enact regulations specific to AI, addressing issues such as bias, transparency, accountability, and safety. However, striking the right balance between fostering innovation and safeguarding societal interests remains a challenge.

- **International Cooperation**: Given the global nature of AI, international cooperation and collaboration are crucial for establishing harmonized standards and frameworks that promote ethical AI development and deployment.

In conclusion, addressing the ethical considerations and challenges associated with AI, including bias, fairness, privacy, and regulation, is essential for realizing the full potential of AI while ensuring that it benefits society as a whole. By fostering transparency, accountability, and inclusivity in AI development and deployment, we can build a future where AI technologies serve the common good and uphold fundamental human values.

Chapter 6
Reinforcement Learning and Autonomous Systems

Reinforcement Learning (RL) represents a paradigm of machine learning where an agent learns to interact with an environment to achieve a goal through trial and error. In this chapter, we explore the principles of RL, its applications in various domains, and the challenges and future directions in the field.

Markov Decision Processes and Q-Learning

Reinforcement Learning is based on the framework of Markov Decision Processes (MDPs), which model decision-making problems in stochastic environments.

- **Markov Decision Processes**: MDPs consist of states, actions, transition probabilities, rewards, and a discount factor. The agent's goal is to learn a policy that maximizes the expected cumulative reward over time.

- **Q-Learning**: Q-Learning is a model-free RL algorithm that learns an optimal action-value function (Q-function) by iteratively updating Q-values based on observed transitions and rewards. It enables the agent to make decisions without explicitly modeling the environment dynamics.

Applications in Robotics, Gaming, and Self-Driving Cars

Reinforcement Learning has found numerous applications in real-world scenarios, including robotics, gaming, and autonomous vehicles.

- **Robotics**: RL is used to train robots to perform complex tasks such as manipulation, navigation, and assembly in dynamic environments. RL enables robots to adapt to changing conditions and learn from experience.
- **Gaming**: RL algorithms have achieved remarkable success in mastering complex games, such as chess, Go, and video games. Deep RL

approaches, such as Deep Q-Networks (DQN) and AlphaGo, have surpassed human performance in challenging games.

- **Self-Driving Cars**: RL plays a crucial role in training autonomous vehicles to navigate traffic, make lane changes, and avoid obstacles. RL algorithms learn optimal driving policies through simulations and real-world trials, leading to safer and more efficient transportation systems.

Challenges and Future Directions in Reinforcement Learning

Despite its successes, RL faces several challenges that limit its applicability and scalability in real-world settings.

- **Sample Efficiency**: RL algorithms often require a large number of interactions with the environment to learn effective policies, making them inefficient for tasks with high-dimensional or continuous action spaces.
- **Generalization and Transfer Learning**: RL agents struggle to generalize knowledge learned in one

environment to new, unseen environments. Transfer learning techniques aim to address this limitation by leveraging knowledge from related tasks or domains.

- **Safety and Ethical Concerns**: RL agents trained in simulated or virtual environments may exhibit unsafe or unethical behavior when deployed in the real world. Ensuring the safety and ethical behavior of autonomous systems remains a significant challenge.

Despite these challenges, RL holds immense potential for advancing AI and enabling autonomous systems to operate in complex and uncertain environments. Future research directions include developing more sample-efficient algorithms, improving generalization and transfer learning capabilities, and addressing safety and ethical concerns to realize the full benefits of RL in real-world applications.

Chapter 7

AI for Good: Solving Global Challenges

Artificial Intelligence (AI) has the potential to address some of the world's most pressing challenges, from humanitarian aid and disaster response to environmental sustainability and healthcare. In this chapter, we explore how AI is being leveraged to tackle these global issues and make a positive impact on society.

AI in Humanitarian Aid and Disaster Response

During humanitarian crises and natural disasters, timely and effective response efforts are crucial to saving lives and minimizing damage. AI technologies offer innovative solutions to enhance disaster preparedness, response, and recovery efforts.

- **Early Warning Systems**: AI-powered early warning systems analyze data from various sources, including satellite imagery, social media, and sensor networks, to detect and predict natural disasters such as hurricanes, earthquakes, and wildfires. These systems enable authorities to issue timely alerts and evacuate at-risk populations.
- **Disaster Damage Assessment**: AI algorithms can analyze aerial and satellite imagery to assess the extent of damage caused by disasters and prioritize rescue and recovery efforts. This helps humanitarian organizations allocate resources more efficiently and effectively.
- **Supply Chain Optimization**: AI optimization algorithms can optimize supply chain logistics during humanitarian aid delivery, ensuring that essential supplies reach affected areas quickly and efficiently.

Environmental Sustainability and Climate Change Mitigation

Addressing climate change and promoting environmental sustainability are among the most significant challenges facing humanity. AI technologies offer innovative solutions to monitor, mitigate, and adapt to the impacts of climate change.

- **Climate Modeling and Prediction**: AI-powered climate models leverage vast amounts of data to simulate complex climate systems, predict future climate trends, and assess the potential impacts of climate change on ecosystems and societies.
- **Renewable Energy Optimization**: AI algorithms optimize the integration and management of renewable energy sources, such as solar and wind power, into the electricity grid, maximizing energy efficiency and reducing greenhouse gas emissions.
- **Environmental Monitoring and Conservation**: AI-enabled monitoring systems, including satellite imagery analysis and acoustic sensors, help track deforestation, wildlife populations, and illegal activities such as poaching and illegal fishing. These systems support conservation efforts and promote sustainable resource management.

Healthcare and Disease Diagnosis

AI has the potential to revolutionize healthcare by improving disease diagnosis, treatment planning, and patient care, ultimately saving lives and reducing healthcare costs.

- **Medical Imaging Analysis**: AI algorithms analyze medical images, such as X-rays, MRI scans, and histopathology slides, to assist radiologists and pathologists in detecting and diagnosing diseases, including cancer, cardiovascular conditions, and neurological disorders.
- **Drug Discovery and Development**: AI accelerates the drug discovery process by predicting the efficacy and safety of potential drug candidates, identifying novel drug targets, and optimizing clinical trial designs. These advancements enable faster and more cost-effective drug development, leading to better treatments for patients.
- **Personalized Medicine**: AI-driven predictive models analyze patient

data, including genetic information, medical history, and lifestyle factors, to tailor treatment plans and interventions to individual patients' unique characteristics and needs. Personalized medicine improves treatment outcomes and reduces adverse effects.

By harnessing the power of AI for humanitarian aid, environmental sustainability, and healthcare, we can address some of the world's most complex challenges and create a better future for generations to come. However, it is essential to ensure that AI technologies are developed and deployed ethically, responsibly, and inclusively to maximize their positive impact on society.

Chapter 8

The Future of AI: Trends and Speculations

As Artificial Intelligence (AI) continues to advance at a rapid pace, shaping the future of technology and society, several key trends and developments are emerging on the horizon. In this chapter, we explore some of the most significant trends and speculations that may shape the future of AI.

Quantum Computing and AI

Quantum computing holds the potential to revolutionize AI by vastly accelerating computation and unlocking new possibilities for solving complex problems.

- **Quantum Machine Learning**: Quantum algorithms and quantum machine learning techniques are being developed to leverage the computational power of quantum computers for tasks such as optimization, pattern recognition, and simulation. Quantum machine learning could enable breakthroughs in drug discovery, materials science, and cryptography.

- **Quantum Neural Networks**: Quantum neural networks, which utilize quantum states to represent and process data, are being explored as a novel approach to building AI systems with unprecedented capabilities. These networks could enable faster training and inference, as well as improved performance on certain types of tasks.

Explainable AI: Making Algorithms Understandable

As AI systems become increasingly complex and opaque, there is a growing need for transparency and interpretability to ensure trust, accountability, and ethical decision-making.

- **Interpretable Models**: Researchers are developing techniques to make AI models more interpretable, allowing humans to understand how decisions are made and why certain outcomes are predicted. This includes methods for visualizing model internals, extracting explanations from black-box models, and quantifying model uncertainty.

- **Ethical and Regulatory Implications**: Explainable AI has important ethical and regulatory implications, particularly in high-stakes domains such as healthcare, finance, and criminal justice. Ensuring that AI systems are transparent and accountable is essential for addressing concerns about bias, fairness, and discrimination.

The Emergence of Artificial General Intelligence (AGI)

Artificial General Intelligence (AGI), sometimes referred to as "strong AI," is the hypothetical AI system that possesses general cognitive abilities comparable to those of humans.

- **Progress Towards AGI**: While current AI systems excel at narrow, domain-specific tasks, achieving AGI remains a long-term goal that requires advancements in areas such as cognitive science, neuroscience, and machine learning. Researchers are exploring novel approaches, including neurosymbolic AI and hierarchical reinforcement learning, to bridge the gap between narrow AI and AGI.

- **Ethical and Societal Implications**: The prospect of AGI raises profound ethical, societal, and existential questions about the future of humanity. Ensuring that AGI is developed and deployed safely, ethically, and responsibly is paramount to mitigate risks and maximize benefits.

Ethical Considerations in Future AI Development

As AI technologies continue to evolve and proliferate, it is essential to prioritize ethical considerations to ensure that AI is developed and deployed in a manner that aligns with human values and promotes the common good.

- **Ethical AI Principles**: Organizations, governments, and industry stakeholders are developing ethical AI principles and guidelines to guide responsible AI development and deployment. These principles address issues such as fairness, transparency, accountability, privacy, and societal impact.

- **Bias Mitigation and Fairness**: Efforts to mitigate bias and promote fairness in AI systems are essential to address disparities and discrimination in decision-making. Techniques such as fairness-aware machine learning, algorithmic auditing, and diversity in dataset collection are crucial for building fair and equitable AI systems.

- **International Collaboration and Governance**: International collaboration and cooperation are essential to establish global norms, standards, and regulations for AI development and deployment. Multistakeholder engagement, inclusive policymaking processes, and ethical oversight mechanisms can help ensure that AI benefits society while minimizing risks and harms.

In summary, the future of AI holds immense promise and potential, but it also poses significant challenges and uncertainties. By staying informed, engaged, and proactive, stakeholders can work together to shape a future where AI serves humanity's best interests and contributes to a more equitable, sustainable, and prosperous world.

Chapter 9

Building Your AI Journey

Embarking on a journey in Artificial Intelligence (AI) and Machine Learning (ML) is an exciting and rewarding endeavor. In this chapter, we explore the essential components of building your AI journey, including education and skill development, tools and frameworks, and the value of collaborative projects and open-source communities.

Education and Skill Development in AI and Machine Learning

Education is the foundation of any successful AI journey. Whether you're a beginner or an experienced professional, continuous learning and skill development are essential to stay updated with the latest advancements in AI and ML.

- **Foundational Knowledge**: Start by building a solid understanding of the fundamentals of AI and ML, including concepts such as data preprocessing, supervised and unsupervised learning, neural networks, and model evaluation.

- **Online Courses and Tutorials**: There are numerous online courses and tutorials available that cover a wide range of AI and ML topics. Platforms like Coursera, edX, Udacity, and Khan Academy offer courses taught by leading experts in the field.

- **Books and Resources**: Supplement your learning with textbooks, research papers, and online resources that delve deeper into specific AI and ML topics. Recommended books include "Deep Learning" by Ian Goodfellow, Yoshua Bengio, and Aaron Courville, and "Hands-On Machine Learning with Scikit-Learn, Keras, and TensorFlow" by Aurélien Géron.

Tools and Frameworks for AI Development

AI development requires access to robust tools and frameworks that streamline the process of building, training, and deploying AI models.

- **Programming Languages**: Python is the predominant programming language for AI and ML development due to its simplicity, versatility, and extensive ecosystem of libraries and frameworks, including NumPy, pandas, scikit-learn, TensorFlow, and PyTorch.
- **Deep Learning Frameworks**: Deep learning frameworks such as TensorFlow, PyTorch, Keras, and MXNet provide high-level APIs for building and training neural networks, as well as low-level capabilities for advanced customization and optimization.
- **Development Environments**: IDEs (Integrated Development Environments) such as Jupyter Notebook, PyCharm, and Visual Studio Code offer powerful tools for writing, debugging, and experimenting with AI code.

Collaborative Projects and Open Source Communities

Collaborative projects and engagement with open-source communities are invaluable for gaining practical experience, sharing knowledge, and building a professional network in the AI and ML field.

- **Kaggle Competitions**: Participating in Kaggle competitions allows you to tackle real-world AI challenges, collaborate with other data scientists, and learn from top performers' strategies and solutions.
- **Open Source Contributions**: Contributing to open-source AI projects on platforms like GitHub is an excellent way to hone your skills, gain exposure to real-world codebases, and make meaningful contributions to the AI community.
- **Online Forums and Communities**: Engage with AI enthusiasts, researchers, and practitioners in online forums and communities such as Stack Overflow, Reddit (e.g., r/MachineLearning), and AI-specific Slack channels. These platforms offer opportunities to ask questions, share

insights, and network with like-minded individuals.

By investing in education and skill development, leveraging powerful tools and frameworks, and actively participating in collaborative projects and open-source communities, you can accelerate your AI journey and contribute to the advancement of AI and ML technologies. Remember that learning is a continuous process, so stay curious, keep exploring, and never stop innovating.

Chapter 10

Conclusion: Embracing the AI Odyssey

As we conclude our exploration of the vast landscape of Artificial Intelligence (AI), it's essential to reflect on the journey we've taken, the impacts AI has had on society, and the imperative to shape a future that harnesses its potential responsibly and inclusively.

Reflections on the Evolution of AI and Its Impacts

The evolution of AI has been nothing short of remarkable. From its humble beginnings as a theoretical concept to its current state as a transformative force shaping every aspect of our lives, AI has made unprecedented strides in a remarkably short period.

We've witnessed the rise of powerful AI technologies such as deep learning, which have revolutionized industries ranging from healthcare and finance to transportation and entertainment. AI-powered systems are now capable of feats once thought impossible, from diagnosing diseases with greater accuracy than human doctors to driving cars autonomously through busy city streets.

However, with these advancements come significant challenges. AI has raised concerns about job displacement, privacy violations, bias and fairness, and the ethical implications of autonomous decision-making. It's imperative that we address these challenges head-on and ensure that AI technologies are developed and deployed in a manner that serves the best interests of humanity.

Call to Action: Shaping a Responsible and Inclusive AI Future

As stewards of AI technology, we have a collective responsibility to shape its future in a way that reflects our values and priorities. This requires a concerted effort from policymakers, industry leaders, researchers, and society as a whole to ensure that AI is developed and deployed responsibly, ethically, and inclusively.

We must prioritize transparency, accountability, and fairness in AI systems, ensuring that they are explainable, auditable, and free from bias and discrimination. We must also safeguard individuals' privacy and data rights, establishing robust regulations and governance frameworks that protect against misuse and abuse.

Moreover, we must ensure that the benefits of AI are equitably distributed across society, bridging the digital divide and addressing disparities in access to technology and opportunity. By fostering diversity and inclusion in the AI workforce and actively engaging marginalized communities in AI development, we can create a future where everyone has a seat at the table.

The Endless Possibilities and Limitless Potential of Artificial Intelligence

Despite the challenges and uncertainties that lie ahead, the future of AI is filled with endless possibilities and limitless potential. AI has the power to augment human intelligence, unlock new frontiers of knowledge, and address some of the most pressing challenges facing humanity, from climate change and healthcare to education and poverty alleviation.

By embracing the AI odyssey with a spirit of collaboration, innovation, and responsibility, we can harness the transformative power of AI to build a better world for generations to come. Let us seize this opportunity to shape a future where AI serves as a force for good, empowering individuals, enriching communities, and advancing the collective well-being of humanity.

Together, let us embark on this journey with optimism, curiosity, and determination, knowing that the future of AI is ours to shape.

www.ingramcontent.com/pod-product-compliance
Lightning Source LLC
LaVergne TN
LVHW051620050326
832903LV00033B/4592